T0353783

Under His Wings

The story of a Soviet girl who overcame numerous obstacles.
The purpose of this story is to encourage young women
to never give up and to keep going in life, no matter what.

ANGELIKA NOVA

Copyright © 2024 Angelika Nova.

All rights reserved. No part of this book may be used or reproduced by any means, graphic, electronic, or mechanical, including photocopying, recording, taping or by any information storage retrieval system without the written permission of the author except in the case of brief quotations embodied in critical articles and reviews.

This book is a work of non-fiction. Unless otherwise noted, the author and the publisher make no explicit guarantees as to the accuracy of the information contained in this book and in some cases, names of people and places have been altered to protect their privacy.

WestBow Press books may be ordered through booksellers or by contacting:

WestBow Press
A Division of Thomas Nelson & Zondervan
1663 Liberty Drive
Bloomington, IN 47403
www.westbowpress.com
844-714-3454

Because of the dynamic nature of the Internet, any web addresses or links contained in this book may have changed since publication and may no longer be valid. The views expressed in this work are solely those of the author and do not necessarily reflect the views of the publisher, and the publisher hereby disclaims any responsibility for them.

Any people depicted in stock imagery provided by Getty Images are models, and such images are being used for illustrative purposes only.
Certain stock imagery © Getty Images.

Interior Image Credit: Natali Gzoim

Instagram Account:
@Nata_Gzoim

www.underhiswingsbook.com

Scripture quotations are taken from the Holy Bible, NEW INTERNATIONAL VERSION®, NIV® Copyright © 1973, 1978, 1984, 2011 by Biblica, Inc.® Used by permission. All rights reserved worldwide.

ISBN: 979-8-3850-2879-5 (sc)
ISBN: 979-8-3850-2880-1 (e)

Library of Congress Control Number: 2024914141

Print information available on the last page.

WestBow Press rev. date: 08/21/2024

WESTBOW
PRESS®
A DIVISION OF THOMAS NELSON
& ZONDERVAN

Table of Contents

Dedication

This book is dedicated to my precious three daughters, who are beautiful inside and out. I hope they will one day read this book and truly understand that God is with them wherever they are.

Also, a special "Thank You" to my loving and always supportive husband.

Thank you to all my dear friends that the Lord has placed on my path in the past years and present time. I love you all dearly. Thank you to all my readers. I appreciate your support and I hope that you will find this book inspiring.

The stories in this book reflect the author's recollection of events. Some names, locations, and identifying characteristics have been changed to protect the privacy of those depicted. Dialogue has been re-created from memory.

Prologue

How many break-ups should a woman undergo to find "the one true love?" And how do we know which relationship is true love that will last a lifetime?

The Bible and our world teach us so differently that this is a question to navigate.

Having three daughters of my own and myself following the world's way earlier in life, I am now holding a position to teach my girls to follow the Bible's way and wait to have an intimate relationship with a man after they get married. My job as a mom is to teach my girls what God says about it and also share with them the mistakes I've made. I also know that it will always be their choice to follow the Bible or not. The only truth is that if I had chosen to follow the Bible early on, I wouldn't have so many hurts in my young adult life.

So, which one is the right way to do it? Looking at my personal life and the lives of those around me, I can honestly say the world's way is a heavy load because it brings unease to a relationship and a future marriage. I only know a few people who have done it God's way and waited until marriage. Their marriages are built on a solid foundation and thriving.

So, do you marry your first love in a pure white dress? Does it mean that a woman's first love needs to be a marriage? The Bible says that our bodies are holy temples, and we are to stay pure until we are married. In 2024, women rarely wait until marriage to have an intimate relationship. But not such a long time ago, in some different cultures, it was a shame to be intimate with someone before marriage. It was even more shameful to get pregnant and not be married. The world's views change constantly with each generation. Today, it is almost acceptable to do as you wish. But the Bible tells us differently. God's word in the Bible never changes. I hope and pray for every young lady and my daughters who might read this book: do not doubt God's message for us. We will never understand its true meaning, but trusting the Lord and his word is the right way to live.

Chapter 1

Marriage

I lay on the cheap linoleum floor, crying and screaming for help. I begged him to stop, but he continued kicking me with his legs on my stomach, my sides, and all over my fragile 21-year-old body. He was entirely out of control; only the devil had his soul at that moment. He was in a stage of rage because it was around 11 pm, and I just got home after going out with my friends. He was screaming at me, "You are worthless; I'll show you how not to obey my rules of marriage."

My grandmother Maria stood in the room watching. I yelled to her, "Please call the police!" She stood covering her face with her palms in tears and shock. She tried to stop Max from finishing what he was doing, but his rage and anger were in control. Maria kept screaming at Max to stop. He finally stopped hitting me, slammed the front door, and left.

My grandmother, Maria, was scared to call the police. And still today, I can't understand why. I often think that if I hadn't had my grandmother close by, if I hadn't had my one-year-old baby girl crying in the bedroom, he might have beaten me until my last breath.

I lay on the kitchen floor with thoughts that my life was over. I cried so hard that I thought all the neighbors could hear me in our apartment building, but no one came to help, and no one called the police. I was in so much pain I could not feel my entire body, but the pain in my soul was much stronger and more difficult to bear. I couldn't believe what he did to me. My brain couldn't comprehend that the man I loved was so mean and evil toward me.

As I slowly tried to get up from the floor, my grandmother helped me. She walked me to her room, and we cried until I finally settled down.

At that time, I lived with my grandmother Maria. After Max left, Maria supported me and helped me care for my one-year-old daughter, Victoria. I was still a full-time student in technical college and couldn't work and support myself. My grandmother fed us on her tiny retirement of around 200 dollars a month.

After this incident, I was so scared that Max would come back home and beat me up again, but he didn't. He started to use mental abuse. He called me on the home phone. When I answered, he called me names and screamed, "Are you still scared of me? You better be because I'll get you one day and slowly cut your pretty face so no other men can enjoy it ever again." His mental abuse continued for several weeks, and finally, he stopped calling and disappeared for a few months.

I was still living in so much fear and terror that every time I entered the apartment building entrance, I looked around and behind me and then slowly walked to my second floor. Even if I just heard his name from other people, my body would start shaking, and I felt nauseated. I didn't want to hear or see him ever again.

Today, as I am writing this chapter of my past, I still cry. I no longer hate Max. I have just an empty and sad feeling toward him. In the 20 years since that incident, God took all my pain away from me. I prayed for years that God would remove my anger, bitterness, and hate. I hated him so much that it started affecting my life with negativity and pessimism. I felt utterly unwanted and lonely, thinking I would never find happiness in this life. Yes, I had some friends who always supported me, but at the end of every day, I was alone with my thoughts and the pain of my broken spirit.

But what did I expect of my sinful relationship with Max since we only got married because I got pregnant? Yes, at that time, we loved each other and had a long-distance relationship between Russia and Latvia, which was very romantic. But the reality was that he was a citizen of Russia and needed to have permanent residency in Latvia. Our only choice was living between his parents' apartment and my grandmother's. We couldn't afford to live separately like many other young couples in the formal USSR countries. Living with parents is normal since there are no alternatives for low class people. But, I had a summerhouse, and on the weekends, we escaped there and enjoyed nature, shashliki (BBQ), and many beautiful flowers that my mom loved to grow. It was always refreshing, and I was happy with the simple and primitive summer home that my dad had built.

Thinking of my parents helped me cope with my situation. Since they were already gone when all the abuse was happening, I had no one to share it with. Often, physical abuse is perceived in Latvia as pretty much a social norm in a family. Society lets men get away with many cruel things toward their families. In my most challenging days, I always asked myself, "Is this the life my mom and dad wanted for me? Is this the marriage that my mom and dad would like to see their daughter live happily ever after? Would my mom give me life so I would be so unhappy?" And I always had an answer in my head: "No"! My life was given to me by my loving parents and the Lord. And I don't have to live with an abuser. It is my life, and I love it. Girls, remember this forever. Don't allow anyone to mistreat you, pray and walk away. Don't hold hate; release it to the Lord and forgive, and God will cover you with his peace. He will bring your joy back someday; you have to believe it.

Several months passed since Max left, and I continued to live with my baby girl, Victoria, and grandmother, Maria. I slowly recovered, was still going to college, and decided to apply for divorce. I told my grandma Maria that I would never forgive Max for everything he had done to me. I don't think I shared with her all the details of everything that was going on, but she supported my decision to divorce. I waited until I received my student monthly allowance of $28 and submitted a divorce application to the court for $10.

Slowly, everything settled down, and I had not heard from him for several months. I knew he was living with his parents in their three-bedroom apartment in a nicer area of Riga. His mother, Lydia, always seemed so nice to me, but I couldn't understand why she never even called to ask how I or baby Victoria were doing. His dad, Pavel, was a retired marine officer and had always been a serious man who had problems with alcohol. Sometimes, I thought, how could that family not care about me or my baby girl? At that time, I did not work, and my grandma supported me financially from her tiny monthly retirement pension, about $200 a month. So, all 3 of us lived on potatoes and bread.

Years later, by growing in my faith, I know why my marriage didn't work out. I brought all my sin into it, and he brought his. I dated other guys before him, even during our dating period when he lived in Russia, and I lived in Latvia. My marriage had sin from the beginning. We didn't know how to have a Godly marriage and how to treasure and respect each other. He often left me and our baby home and was gone for a few nights. It was usual for him to hang out with his buddies and drink somewhere. I was very unhappy with such treatment, his drinking, and his constant jealousy. But I wasn't an angel myself. Once, I kissed a married man while I was married. God tells us we are committing a sin only by thinking about it, and here it is!

Even more so, after I found out that I was pregnant with our 2nd baby, I made the decision not to have another child. A few of my friends already had abortions before the age of 21. So, young people looked at it in Latvia like it wasn't a big deal. I didn't have a strong faith either at that time or a church that would be supportive of me and tell me that it was such a big sin and that I would regret the decision for the rest of my life. I had none of it.

I know it was my choice in the end, but I also blame the socialized medicine that allowed us young women to have abortions so quickly and completely free. All it took was one visit to my OBGYN and her cold and direct question to me," Giving birth or having an abortion?" There was no encouragement to keep the baby at all. So, by the next week, I was sitting in the lifeline in the clinic's "hallway of shame" with other young moms waiting for my turn. I remember shaking like a leaf as they put me under anesthesia. And the only thing I can remember is waking up and crying out in sorrow for my deceased mom, " Mom, please take my baby boy."

After the day I ended my pregnancy, I felt so empty and ashamed of that decision. It seemed the right choice at that time since we barely had any money to live on. After that day, my already shaky marriage just continued to fall further apart more and more. I felt God was so disappointed and angry with me for what I did.

The Lord is my rock,

my fortress and my deliverer;

my God is my rock, in whom I take refuge,

my shield and the horn of my salvation,

my stronghold.

PSALM 18:2

REFLECTION

*If anything touches your heart today,
let it flow out, and allow God to work within you
to bring you peace and joy.*

Chapter 2

Childhood

I grew up in a big family: my mom, dad, grandma, and two older brothers. We all lived in Riga in a spacious 4-bedroom apartment in the city's center. I used to walk to and from school by myself and especially loved my treats on the way back. I loved getting the frozen lemon sorbet in a paper cup for just eight kopeiki (Russian rubles and kopeiki (coins) was the currency in USSR). I also enjoyed visiting the local bakery for freshly made glazed chocolate eclairs and vanilla pastries. The taste of freshly made chocolate éclair that melted in my mouth is hard to forget.

My childhood was very well-rounded. I took dance and piano classes and sang in the school chorus. Also, my parents often took me to the local theater to watch opera. It was always such a great event when we went to the fancy theater that was decorated in Baroque style. The dark red colored walls with unique art pieces and dark red velvet draperies on the stage created an extravagant atmosphere inside the theater. I loved it when my mom bought me a special occasion velvet dress for the theater and did my hair in a fancy updo. It was fun living in the city. For the most part, I was safe back then. The town was walkable and filled with many shops and cozy street cafes. I could take a trolley, bus, or a tram to any part of town. The architecture was and still is impressive. Many buildings from the Baroque and Art Nouveau eras surround the old city. Riga has charm with many beautiful parks, small, intriguing streets, and fountains. But beyond the old city limits, you see many run-down Stalin's era buildings that serve as apartments that are unfortunately, not so appealing.

We also went to two other places as a family: our lovely summer home, which my dad built outside of Riga, and the village home where my dad's parents lived.

I wouldn't say I liked going to the village home during the summer. It was always a long and boring ride that would take us around four hours. But the best part of the trip was the dessert bakery, where we stopped every time at the halfway mark. I used to buy some fresh-baked vanilla pastries, and they were so good!

The village house where my dad's parents used to live was located very close to the Belarus border, about 200 miles southeast of Riga. In the 1980s, when I was growing up, Latvia was still part of the USSR, and there were official borders between Latvia and Belarus. It was under a socialist regime until it gained independence in 1991.

My family had enough money, a decent car, and food back then. My dad used to drive to Belarus and bring items he could sell in Riga, such as well-made shoes, women's faux and real fur winter coats, and wallpaper. Maybe it was then that I developed my love for interior design. Seeing so much wallpaper in my childhood in all different colors and scales of the traditional Damask pattern played a role in my career. Later, I attended the college for Interior Design and worked as an interior designer in America.

Back in the village countryside, I didn't have many friends, just a few neighbor's kids who would come by our house looking for some extra work. My parents always brought clothes and extra food for them, especially winter shoes, which we found at a second-hand store back in Riga. I would say that my childhood was, for the most part, very good. We were not rich or poor.

So, my summers were simple, sweet, and fun. I cherish those memories in a special place in my heart. We would swim and fish at the lake, run in the orchard, and jump on the hay in the barn.

My grandfather's primitive log house was about 10 minutes away from the main road. It was built by a beautiful lake in the middle of the birch and aspen woods. There was also a small creek with red clay and rocks where I used to play as a child.

Nature was incredible at this tiny home. The fresh air used to fill my lungs with energy, and my toes would tickle as I ran barefoot on the wet grass early in the mornings. I loved visiting the surrounding woods with my mom to pick juicy wild raspberries and mushrooms. We took a blanket and lunch with us and enjoyed our picnic after a long morning picking fruit and mushrooms. Tired, I would lie down to look at the blue sky and watch the funny-looking clouds going by. We were surrounded by nature, birds singing, woodpeckers pecking, and cuckoo sounds. Back home, we compared all the mushrooms and who had the largest porcini bolete or an aspen mushroom.

The best part of being in the village home was the beautiful lake. I often ran down to the lake in the early morning to see if I had caught any crusina carps in my fish trap. I used to swim on the old wooden float with a long stick as the paddle to put my traps into the lake in the evening. My furry black cat, Million, followed me on the small trail through the woods and waited on the dock to see if I had any fresh fish in my traps. Then we would return to the house to the backyard to clean the fish up, and my cat would enjoy fresh fish for breakfast. Swimming was an everyday activity for me in the summer, and I loved jumping off the old wooden dock.

My grandfather and grandmother (my dad's parents) lived in a simple log home. There was no phone, only well water and an outdoor bathroom. There was no shower, so we washed ourselves in the small log cabin in the woods we called our "black Russian sauna house." The interior was pitch black, with only one low-voltage bulb for light. As a young girl, I was terrified to go inside what I called "The Witch House," with all the green moss growing from the old sagging roof and red and white amanita mushrooms surrounding it.

The interior of the village house was straightforward. It had a kitchen with a large cooking stove and one large room serving everyone as one large bedroom and living room. This room's entrance was small, and people had to bend to enter. When we visited my grandfather, we all slept in this one room. It had two beds behind a curtain, a separate sofa bed, and a tall Russian clay stove on top of which you could sleep. That's where I remember my grandfather sleeping.

Near the village house were three other buildings, two hay barns, and one animal barn. My grandfather had three pigs, some chickens, and a cow. I didn't enjoy my daily chore of milking that cow.

My grandfather Yakov was born in 1906. I remember him as a slim, short man with a curved back. I always thought he had a small hump on his back from carrying two metal buckets full of well water on his shoulders using an old wooden balance beam. That's the only way we would bring the water out of the well in the woods to the house. He wore grey pants, a leather belt, and an overly washed white-and-black checkered flannel shirt. I remember his wrinkled face, always smiling at me. If he wasn't working around the house, I could find him resting on the small living room sofa and listening to the old-fashioned radio. He woke up around 5 am each morning, fed the animals, or worked in the garden.

Sometimes, he wore a mask over his face, similar to what people wear in fencing. As a child, I thought he looked strange in the outfit that covered his body from his head to his toes. This is what he wore to get his beehives. It was the best treat to shave the beehives with a knife, put the raw honey on baked white French bread, and eat it with a glass of fresh warm milk from the cow.

As an adult, I often think about who my grandfather was. He was in his mid-30s during World War II, 1942-1945. I can only imagine how much suffering, pain, and agony those times brought to him and his family. He used to tell me stories about German soldiers, but I was too young to remember any of them. I imagine his family had barely any food to eat during those years. I imagine how much suffering he went through with harsh, brutal winters. That area could get so much snow that you could barely walk. I imagine him hearing tanks and shots at night, praying for his safety and the safety of his kids. Despite not knowing the details of his life during the war, I know he was a hero. Maybe I inherited some of his soul strength and incredible inner endurance to carry on through life.

My grandfather had four children, two boys and two girls. His first son was born before 1942 and died at a very young age from diphtheria. My aunt Darya was born in the 1940s, and though she is still alive today, I have no contact with her.

Another aunt, Svetlana, was born in 1942; my dad, Stanislav, was born in 1947.

I never saw my grandfather complain. He was always calm and positive. His simple, peaceful life was enough for him. If I could go back in time, I would sit down with him as a little girl and tell him, "Grandpa, when I grow up, I'll move far, far away to the USA, and I will live in a million-dollar home. Each bedroom will have a private bathroom with a shower and indoor plumbing. My home would be as big as all your four neighbors' homes combined. And then I will marry a prince—well, not quite, but pretty close—and I will have three beautiful daughters." If I could do that, he would have looked at me under his glasses, chuckled, and probably said, "Keep dreaming, girl, keep dreaming big."

Once, in 1991, I saw my grandfather heartbroken. He wept while standing on his fragile knees in front of the black cascade where my 49-year-old aunt Svetlana was lying covered with an old-fashioned piece of lace tulle covering her face. A local Orthodox priest wearing all-black mourning attire shook a golden can of oils around the cascade. The smoke and smell of the essential oils from the golden can make me sick and nauseous. I was only twelve at the time, but the grief and pain on my grandfather's face was hard to bear. I am grateful that Yakov did not live long enough to grieve another of his children just a couple of years later—my dad, Stanislav.

My Aunt Svetlana had been found hanging on her bedroom door handle. Still today, I can't help but wonder why she committed suicide. She was a wonderful aunt, gentle and kind. She left behind her only child, my cousin Karina, who now lives in Germany. Karina and I often talk about our childhood and our parents, and we both know that we survived our young years and became happy in our lives only under enormous grace from God and His protection.

REFLECTION

If anything touches your heart today,
let it flow out, and allow God to work within you
to bring you peace and joy.

Chapter 3

Parents

If I close my eyes and picture my father, I see a tall, medium-weight man with a mustache and good, heartwarming blue eyes surrounded by crow's feet wrinkles from smiling. He wore a winter puffer jacket or natural sheepskin coat and looked handsome in his beaver winter hat. My father was always kind and good to me. I always felt loved by him, and he disciplined me just enough. The best times in my childhood were with my dad in our summer house garage, fixing my old bike, or repainting the wrought iron gate in the summer house. In the winter, he tied a rope behind his car with the sleigh attached to it and swirled me carefully around the roads and corners.

My father grew stricter as I progressed into my teen years. He loved giving me chores to do before I could go out with my friends. One year, our summer house garden was overflowing with snails. So he said, "OK, you can go out after getting a bucket of snails." My friend and I would spend an hour or so collecting the sticky creatures.

I had no doubt I was daddy's girl. I loved being with him, whether selling our village apples and potatoes at the farmers market or selling cars at the Sunday car market. Our life was good until a financial crisis hit Latvia in the 1990s. After this, it was difficult for Dad to find a job to provide for our family. But we managed as a family somehow, and I wasn't sure how my dad provided for us. I had a good relationship with my dad and loved him very much. He was understandably stricter with me during my teen years and wasn't a fan of some of the boys I dated. He never got to meet one very special boy, unfortunately.

In eleventh grade, I met a handsome young man with dark brown eyes, shiny black hair, and a beautiful white smile. His name was Amir, and he was from Beirut, Lebanon. He was a student at a local college. We developed very strong feelings for each other. We didn't officially date, but we were very happy together. We were in love. Amir spoke English, but I managed to communicate with him just with a few English words I knew then.

When I was 17 years old, Amir was the only thing I wanted to think about. Anywhere I went in town, my eyes looked for him. I was ecstatic when we finally told each other, "I love you," one evening. He was the man I dreamed of having a family with. But it all went crashing down fast and hard.

One day, I was planning to go out of town to visit my mom, who was staying at our summer home. The trip was about an hour's ride on a train. The first time I showed up, my train didn't come. The second time, I was late for the train. The third time I finally got on the last train, the conductor put me out because I didn't have a ticket. I sensed God needed me to be home that day, so I went home. That night, I got a phone call from a neighbor's boy from my grandfather's village, where my father had traveled that week. The boy's voice was shaking when he told me that my dad shot himself.

The deepest pain I ever felt in my life was that night. The following day, I could barely open my swollen eyes, but I had to go to our summer home and tell this horrible news to my mom.

The next few months were awful and hard. I was so broken and disappointed with God. I could not understand why God allowed it to happen and what my mom, my brothers, and I were going to do without Dad.

For nine months, I dreamed real, strange dreams about my dad. In them, my dad would come to me and tell me that he was alive. I woke up with a very strange feeling that my dad was close to me and was indeed alive, but this was only in my mind.

After my dad passed away, I never saw Amir again since I was grieving and didn't go anywhere to socialize. Later in the summer, I learned Amir graduated and returned home. His friend told me that he had to go back and get married because he had gotten a girl in his country pregnant. I felt broken and just empty inside, with no faith left in me.

My beautiful mother, Eva, always fixed her gorgeous, long, brown hair on self-made paper rollers at night. The following day, she wanted to look stunning for my dad with wavy, shiny hair. My mother was an artist who loved painting and, interestingly, taking photos of me. She also loved knitting warm sweaters for me and Dad and decorating our summer home and apartments. She was a good cook and made a lot of yummy baked goods for the whole family.

My mom always made our house welcoming and warm, especially for the Christmas and New Year seasons. She prepared a big table with lots of homemade food she made with my dad. The famous Russian potato salad" Olivje" and "Seledka pod shuboj" (salty herring under the shredded layers of boiled beets, carrots, potatoes, and onion) were two main dishes that were always at the celebration table. The crispy oven-baked potatoes, and juicy smoked chicken my dad made were family favorites. And, of course, my mom's famous waffle cake with boiled condensed milk, fruit marmalade, and hazelnuts was my absolute favorite! The smell of clementines and freshly cut Christmas trees (yolka) filled our apartments. My brothers always brought a giant Christmas tree that touched the ceilings, and we enjoyed decorating it with many Christmas ornaments and garlands.

Once, when I was showering my daughter, then eight years old, she said out of nowhere, "Mom, if I didn't have my hair, I wouldn't go to school because I would have to wear a wig." Suddenly, I remembered my mother sitting in her bedroom in front of her large mirror with scissors in her hands. I had just gotten home from school. My mother told me, "Angelika, today you need to cut my hair off." I was in shock. "No, Mom!" I said. "How? Why? Your beautiful hair!" She told me it would fall out soon anyway since she had started chemotherapy. I slowly worked my scissors into her silky hair, wiping away my tears.

I told my daughter, "Honey, there are a lot of people in this world who are bald. And lots of them are sick with cancer. You know honey, my mom was bald at one point in my life."

Why had I been the one to cut it? Why me, who as a teen had already gone through so much? After her chemo started in the next few weeks, my mom was bald. She hid her few hairs under a shiny wig.

After a couple of months, her natural hair started to grow. And it was so cute and thick, so we had fun with her styling it with gel for a hip look.

For a few years, my mother battled Leukemia, going back and forth to hospitals. Doctors would give a blood transfusion and medication and send her home. Months later, she was back in a hospital. I hated that place. Since we lived in a country with socialized medicine, there were long lines to get to a doctor. My mom used to bribe doctors with cash, expensive liquor, or fancy boxes of chocolate to get good pills. While my dad was alive, he took care of my mom. He loved her so much, and I remember him getting very sad every time my mom would need to go back to the hospital. He told me once that he doesn't want to live if my mom dies.

The year 1996 was a tragic year for me and my family.

In November, my mom was again hospitalized. One day, I saw her, and her doctor called me in his office. He told me that they couldn't do anything for my mom anymore. I was devastated. I prayed and prayed to God to heal her, but my endless prayers were not answered the way I wanted. It was the last time I saw my mom in the hospital; I kissed her unconscious body and spoke to her, although I wasn't sure if she could hear me. God never healed my mom on earth. My mom passed away in the hospital a day later; she was only 43 years old. I felt empty, broken, and angry with God for putting me through that. I felt forgotten, cursed, and hopeless. I could not understand why God allowed this tragedy in my life and why I lost both of my parents in one year.

At my mom's funeral, strangely, I wasn't in significant emotional pain. I felt a weird and deep sense of peace that covered my sad mind. I didn't even have money to buy flowers for my mom's funeral. My best friend bought them for me.

Only many years later, after building a deeper relationship with God, was I able to understand that my mother's death was God's hand on me and His answer to my prayers. In His way, He ended my mom's sufferings from both losing her husband and her battle with cancer.

I was only 17 years old when I lost both my parents—that year changed my life forever. There I was without both parents for one year. How could I ever survive these events and not become a drug addict or an alcoholic? Only with God's protection.

"Don't worry about anything, instead pray about everything.

Tell God what you need and thank him for what he has done.

Then you'll experience God's peace that

surpasses all understanding.

His peace will guard your heart and mind

as you live in Christ Jesus".

Philippians 4:6-7

REFLECTION

*If anything touches your heart today,
let it flow out, and allow God to work within you
to bring you peace and joy.*

Chapter 4

Moving to the USA

After my parents passed away, I lived with my grandmother Maria in Riga's 2-bedroom apartment and continued to attend 11th grade.

Maria was in bad health and was having trouble with her legs. Although she was only in her mid-60s, one leg had an open wound that would never heal. She had difficulty walking, and because of the constant bleeding, she was diagnosed with Leukemia, too. She needed to support me on her tiny pension. She bought large bags of potatoes and meat leftovers at the market. She saw my struggles as a teenager, but I never had a deep, loving relationship with her. She always judged me, and often said mean words toward me.

After I told her I was pregnant with Max's baby, my grandmother did not speak to me for months. She didn't want me to have a baby, but God had a different plan.

I had my baby and married Max. As you know, we have had many struggles in our marriage, financially and spiritually. After he abused me, my grandmother supported my divorce. But six months into it, Max begged me to forgive him and start living together again. I accepted, and Maria hated me for my decision, although I probably should've listened to her since I knew deep down inside her she meant well.

We lived together, and she enjoyed my baby girl, Victoria. I know she loved her a lot, and that baby gave her joy. Maria used to buy Victoria chocolate candy and play with her as much as she could. But Maria's health was declining, and after being in a hospital for quite some time, she passed away in 2001.

After her passing, Victoria, Max, and I continued to live in my apartment. We continued to have financial hardship due to a lack of jobs and were barely making it. We didn't have money to pay for the condo any longer, so we decided to sell my 2-bedroom condo and go to the US to work for a year. My best friend Sophia already worked in the USA, and she helped us process the paperwork to go to the USA. Our only option was to leave Victoria with Max's parents, Lydia and Pavel. We planned to go to the USA for no more than a year to make some money and come back to Riga.

My baby Victoria was only three years old when I said goodbye to her. It was a tough decision, but I trusted God had a better future for me.

I remember going to a small Orthodox church near my old condo in Riga, buying candles, and praying at Jesus's icon to keep His hand on my daughter. And He did. I remember buying an icon with His image and leaving it in Victoria's room so it would somehow magically protect her.

During my journey in the USA, Jesus did protect my daughter; He protected her from sickness and any accidents.

After selling my apartment in Latvia, we moved in with my in-laws in Riga. The plan was to leave Victoria for one year with Lydia and Pavel, Max's parents. It was the only option for us to be able to go and work in the USA. What else did I have to lose? I had no job; my ex-husband had no job, and we barely had any money for food and necessities. The opportunity to work in the USA sounded very good since my friend was already making some money there. I felt like it would be a chance for us to have a better life and give Victoria a better quality of life.

I had a good relationship with Lydia and Pavel back then. Except, Pavel had been drinking a lot. There were days when I came home with baby Victoria to find him lying on the stairs in the apartment hallway. I remember one time Lydia had to call an ambulance after Pavel had been drinking for a few weeks. His swollen from drinking face was unrecognizably scary looking. The smell of alcohol throughout the apartment was pronounced, and when the doctor came and asked if he had been drinking, Pavel said, "No." He was confusing me with his daughter and couldn't remember the year it was. Sadly, he had alcoholism, but he never did anything to treat it. He would stop for a few months and then get back to drinking again. At times, I was scared to stay home alone with my baby. I don't know how I could leave my daughter there. But Lydia took good care of Victoria. If Pavel was drinking, they would leave the apartment and live in their summer house away from Pavel.

Max left for the US first, and a few months later, I followed him to Baltimore, Maryland. I was twenty-one when we started to work low-paying jobs at some hotels, cleaning hotel rooms and helping in the kitchens. We lived with five roommates in a two-bedroom condo rented by other immigrants. So we spent the rest of the money I had from selling Maria's apartment without plans to return home.

My husband sank his unhappiness into alcohol, so our relationship was getting worse day by day. I had a lot of stress coping with missing my daughter. I hated not being able to see her. I had to buy a calling card to call her. I worked 12-hour shifts cleaning hotel rooms from 8 am-3 pm and then 4 pm-10 pm, helping as a food runner in a restaurant. My unhappiness took a toll on me, and my "dreamy" life in the USA was crushed by harsh reality. I prayed that God would somehow see my unhappiness and make my life better. I wanted to return home to my daughter so badly, but I couldn't. I had no money and no place to go back to.

After being in Baltimore for a while, we moved to Atlanta, where my best friend Sophia lived. Sophia lived separately from us, about 10 minutes away. And we started living in one rental condo with Sophia's ex-boyfriend, Igor, and her other friend. Max began to work with Igor at his construction business. We didn't have much money, our only furniture was a new mattress, and that was all. My relationship with my husband was declining every day, with him often getting drunk and becoming mean and rude with his frequently offensive comments. I often cried and was afraid to do anything about it.

Igor had separated from his long relationship with Sophia and was lonely and unhappy. He tried to see Sophia to ask if there was any chance they might be together again. During girls' nights out, Sophia often told me and other friends how happy she was with her new American boyfriend. Igor didn't know this yet.

It all started with smiles and occasional eye contact. More and more, I felt distanced and unhappy with my husband and drawn toward Igor. When we all went to the pool, we laughed and played ball together, and it felt good to feel like someone cared for me again. Sometimes, I found fresh flowers in the living room condo and knew they were from Igor for me. Evening conversations were filled with happiness and romance so we couldn't deny it any longer. I was ashamed to tell my best friend I was falling for her ex-boyfriend. I knew it was wrong, but my heart felt relieved with Igor when we hugged. He was my mental escape from the unhappy marriage I was in.

I decided to separate from my husband and wrote him a "goodbye" letter, asking him to let me go forever. I remember giving him this letter and explaining how unhappy I was with him and that I wanted to end our marriage. I stood with Igor in front of him and told him I wanted the divorce and that I was leaving.

As Igor and I drove away, I felt happy and unfortunate at the same time. The next morning, I felt ashamed for kissing Igor.

I was lost, and I decided to return to my ex-husband. He told me he would forgive me and take me back. So we packed our belongings and took the bus to Memphis, Tennessee, to begin our new married life together.

I couldn't call Sophia and tell her everything. It took me the next year or so to write her a letter with all the explanations and ask her to forgive me. She graciously did.

We lived in downtown Memphis, Tennessee, and I worked long days at the Downtown Marriot. I had no car, and I walked to the hotel about 15 minutes. It was not a big deal in the morning since it was daylight. But coming home at 11 pm was scary. Every night, after finishing my work at the restaurant, I put on my long sweater with a hood covering my long blond hair and walked or ran home. The area was filled with people at night lying drunk or overdosed on the streets. I was so scared I prayed, "God, please keep me safe. Please keep me alive today and let me get to my apartment."

My apartment was my safe place back then. It was a tall, old building where we lived with roommates, alone but not quite alone. It was filled with cockroaches, and I covered my ears at night with a blanket while I slept on a floor mattress. When I cooked, cockroaches smelled my food above the stove.

Some immigrant workers we knew had cars and charged me fifty cents for a ride home from the hotel. I wonder now if they got wealthier of that money, ha!

After several months, we decided to move to Michigan, where we were promised a better job. We bought our first car, an old white Mitsubishi Galant, for $500 and a paper road map and started our journey toward a better future again.

Again, things didn't go as well as we hoped. Often, we were without work, or Max would be a driver/supervisor, giving him a sense of authority over the other immigrant workers. Almost every day, he would drink beer, and we would get into a fight. One day, I went to take a bath. I was so sad because of our fights and inability to move on anymore. The thought of suicide crossed my mind. I watched as the water came out from the bath faucet and felt so broken. I didn't want to live.

In a split second, I had a clear thought, "I have to live; I can't stop now; I have a daughter who needs me." I finished my bath and wiped away my tears. Then I packed my backpack with my passport and all the pictures of my baby girl. I knew one day, this emergency bag would come in handy. I didn't care about all the stuff in the apartment since we didn't have much. A mattress on the floor, a shelf with a TV, and a box for a coffee table.

That day came soon. When we fought again, I asked Max, " Why do you think you are better than anyone else?" He stormed toward the shelf, kicked it over, and broke the TV. He yelled cuss words. Panicked, I grabbed my backpack from the closet and ran outside. It was the time to go to work. I told him I would move out today if he'd only let me have the car. I told him he could stay in the apartment and I'd survive somewhere—I just needed a vehicle. He said, "No way you'll have the car, sit down, I take you to work."

I sat down as we drove toward the shopping plaza where I had just started working as a telephone marketer. In the parking lot, he yelled again and told me if I didn't return that night to get my clothes, he'd throw them in the garbage outside the apartment.

I stood shivering from cold and crying, embarrassed to show my tears and pain to my coworkers. And I know now, by the grace of God, I had these good people in my life. Only the Lord can bring people to your path at the right moment when you need them. My boss, Mila, a sweet and caring Romanian lady, knew what I was going through, and that day, she said, "Angelika, you can come live in my house. You don't have to pay rent for now. Everything will be ok."

I stayed there for a few months and felt loved and supported by her two wonderful daughters. Their cute and comfortable home was my safe space where I could be myself again without fear, anxiety, and stress. We spend a lot of time together, and I am forever grateful for all their support, care, and help during those difficult times.

Every day for the next few months, we locked the front office door in fear that Max would come back to hurt me. He called the company, and my coworkers said I wasn't working there anymore and that I moved away to another state. I knew Max was looking for me to apologize and start everything all over again, but I lived in fear that he would find me and kill me. His parents knew that we had separated. Often, when I called them and asked to talk to Victoria, they were mean to me and always blamed me for everything. They threatened they wouldn't let me speak to Victoria if I didn't send money. Which I did every month anyway, but it was an emotionally challenging time for me to deal with their cruel talks.

I prayed so much for the Lord to show me the way from then on. I told God that if only he would help me find a small place to live, I would leave Max and never return to him.

The Lord heard me and answered my prayer. One day, a girl in my office brought me three bags of clothes. I had my emergency backpack, passport, Victoria's photos, and $1 in my pocket. She said," Hey, Angelika, I have a friend leaving the US in a few months. She is looking for a roommate to take over her lease and some of her housekeeping jobs." I immediately told her, "Yes, I am very interested." It was another grace of God leading me in my path and showing me the way.

"Fear is a liar," just like in the song by Zach Williams. It will destroy you if you don't get a hold of it, and the only way to fight you fear to pray for God to take away your fears. And he will do it, no matter where you are! He did it for me; he will do it for you! God slowly led me into my new life path, and my fears faded.

"For I, the Lord your God, hold your right hand;

It is I who say to you,

"Fear not, I am the one who helps you"

Isaiah 41:13

Chapter 5

Repentance

After I broke up with my ex-husband, I found a room to live in and a good house-cleaning job. Also, I still worked at a phone company. A few months after I moved, I found a spare car key and remembered that the title of our car was in my name. One winter night, my friends and I returned to the old apartment where my husband lived and excitedly drove my car away. I knew he was mad the following day when he showed up in the parking lot, but the car was not there. My roommates told me later he broke a wall inside the apartment. But I felt like it was my revenge to take what was mine.

It had been almost four years since I had seen my baby Victoria. FaceTime did not exist in 2004. I remember when I felt there was no way out and was lost. I was very lonely, not officially divorced yet, and tired of my job of cleaning homes and coming back to the run-down apartments. I was spiritually broken.

I worked so hard and saved all my money. In my head, I was debating whether to return to Latvia. But there was nothing there, no apartment to live in. The money I made wasn't enough to buy a place. I could get to Victoria and move to Ireland, where two of my brothers lived. But I was so used to America by then and saw how much potential the country had for people who worked hard. Although I had to work low-paying jobs such as cleaning hotel rooms, house cleaning, working as a waitress, and babysitting, I still could afford to pay for my apartment, food, and gas and save some money to support Victoria in Riga. If I would go back to Riga, there are no opportunities for me. I would start where I left off, and all my hard work in the USA would never pay off. I knew Victoria would have a much better life in the USA, and I could provide for her. I wanted to bring my daughter Victoria to America.

One night, I kneeled, prayed, and cried with my open soul, asking God to forgive me for whatever I did wrong. I prayed for HIS grace and mercy and for him to help me have my daughter back soon. I named all the people from my past that I thought I had wronged. I asked God to forgive me for my mistakes and lead me into the future with his firm guidance.

I asked God to help me find a nice man and have a good family. I prayed to see my daughter Victoria soon. Now, almost 18 years later, I know that it was my repentance that led me to turn my life around for good. Only the Lord can move things and make them happen. From that point forward, everything in my life became much better.

That night, God lifted me after I repented of all my sins, and from that point on, God has always been with me.

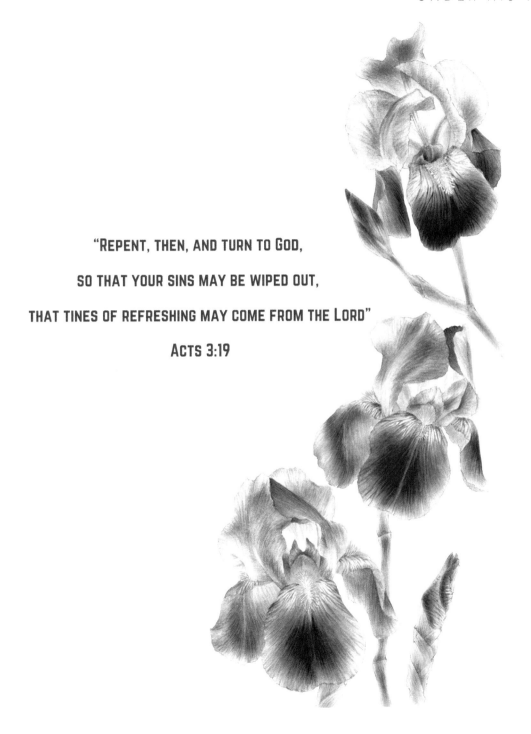

"Repent, then, and turn to God,

so that your sins may be wiped out,

that tines of refreshing may come from the Lord"

Acts 3:19

REFLECTION

If anything touches your heart today,
let it flow out, and allow God to work within you
to bring you peace and joy.

Love.

"Happy 15th anniversary to my husband Edward, whom I love dearly.

With all of our ups and downs, I still want to be married to you, and I cannot imagine having anyone else beside me. I know you were the answer to my prayer back then when I lived in my small apartment after escaping from my ex-husband. You are the answer to my prayers."

A few months later, after that night of confessing to the Lord and repenting, I visited my friend Sophia in Atlanta, where I met Edward. We went out with a few friends, and Edward was the guy I had a crush on immediately. He liked me right away, too. He was 40 years old, a handsome single man with a bald head and warm blue eyes. I was in Atlanta for only a few days, but that time allowed us to get to know each other. We had dinner with our friends, and the next day, we saw each other again at a restaurant and went to the aquarium. I told him that I had a daughter in Latvia, I stayed on an expired student visa, and I was going away to Ireland soon. Besides that, I was still legally married to my ex, and he didn't want to give me a divorce.

When my time came to go back from Atlanta to Michigan, I remember Edward taking me to the airport and taking my suitcase. And when I was looking at him, I saw something more than just a guy I just met.

I sat down in my airplane seat and started to cry. Unexplained feelings of joy and warmth came to me, and I knew something was happening by meeting Edward.

We dated long-distance for a while—him in Atlanta and me in Michigan. We talked on the phone for hours in the evenings and missed each other a lot. I flew back to Atlanta several times, and he flew to Michigan. And just a few months after we met, he took me to LA to meet his parents. I met my future mother-in-law and father-in-law. They were such friendly and warm people. I couldn't believe it the way they treated me. When we left their home, I told Nicolle, "I just wanted to tell you that you raised such an amazing man." Edward later said to me that it was after that he knew I'd be his wife one day.

After about six months of dating, I moved to Atlanta and temporarily lived with Sophia and her friend. I finally became legally divorced, and my relationship with Edward grew stronger.

We got much closer after I moved to Atlanta and were happy together. One day, he told me that he loved me, and I was so excited to hear that because I loved him too. He used to make silly videos of me, and we would mail the tape to Victoria so she could see me. He photoshopped her photos with mine so I could at least have a picture of me and Victoria together. But he also often saw me so unhappy when I called Victoria. I cried a lot and had nightmares from not seeing my daughter for so long. I wanted to be with her.

Our relationship became more serious, and we started discussing possibly getting married. We had so much fun looking at engagement rings and custom-ordered one for me. So, one day, Edward surprised me by taking me to Jekyll Island for a weekend. We went on a beach walk the first night and had a great time together. We sat down on some large rocks by the dunes, and suddenly, Edward was on one knee in front of me. He held my hands and said, "Angelika, the love of my life. I am so happy that we met. I could not be happier with you. Will you marry me?" And he got a ring box and opened it. I saw a giant 5-carat stone and said, "Edward, it is not my ring!" He laughed, and I understood he was tricking me with a fake ring to have fun. Then he got my actual engagement ring that we ordered. I was so happy and could not believe that I was engaged.

Shortly after, we went to court, just the two of us, and got married. It was mainly for the paperwork that I needed to start processing so I could return to Riga soon. Several months later, we got married in front of the Lord on a beautiful lake in Arkansas. I wore a gorgeous wedding dress and a veil. Although neither my brothers nor Victoria could be there with me that day, I felt so happy!

That's where my happily ever after started. The Lord was with us along the way.

I remember Edward and I holding hands together and praying that God would guide us to get Victoria to the US safely. We prayed for my travel to Riga. We prayed for the paperwork to go smoothly, and although it took seven months to get Victoria's visa, it was always under God's caring hand. The Lord helped us with everything.

Here I was, five years after coming to the USA, finally able to go back to get my daughter!

When the time came for me to return to Riga and get Victoria, I did not tell Lydia I was coming. I feared she would try to take Victoria away. A couple of days before my trip, I called Victoria and told her that Mommy was coming home. That way, I thought they would not have a lot of time to plan anything. I still remember Victoria's voice crying on the phone, saying, "Mommy, is it true? Do you promise that you are coming? Is it true?"

Traveling to Riga was scary, nerve-racking, and exciting at the same time. I was inside the airplane, taking off to the unknown. But God always had his hand on me. I sat by a Christian man all my flight. He was traveling on a mission trip to Africa. He held my hand and prayed before every meal. Looking back 20 years later, I know it was God's angel sent to me personally who supported me during the trip to Latvia and kept me calm.

The moment I saw Victoria at the airport, she was exactly like in the last photo I saw of her: tall and cute, with two long blonde braids and a happy smile to see her mommy. We bonded so quickly that no one could separate us.

My ex-in-laws were not nice to me in Riga. We started a huge fight, and I knew I had to take Victoria and find an apartment to live in.

I remember praying, "Lord, I need to find a place to leave today," God helped me again!

That was the day I took charge of my daughter, and although I was shaking like a leaf, in fear that Pavel would hit me at some point, I stood up for myself. I know God was watching over me, and he had his hand on me. I always knew it.

I found an apartment the same day. Coincidence? Nope. Lots of times, people in life say, "Oh, you were so lucky." But looking back, I know in my heart that only God could orchestrate it for me.

If you don't seek God, you will never find him, and you will never experience the life and calmness he has for us. The Lord was with me all seven months during my stay in Riga. That was how long it took to process the visa for Victoria to return to the US.

When I moved out of Lydia's place into an apartment, she told Victoria that her dad, Max, would never call her again because her mommy was taking her away from her home. This was not true. Lydia always knew where we were for the next seven months, and she came to visit us, too. Victoria still went to the same school, too. I never heard Lydia or Pavel apologize for these actions.

Sometimes, I ask Victoria if she remembers any of this, and she says, "Nope." That is a good thing!

After spending seven months in Riga and waiting for the immigration paperwork, Victoria and I arrived in the US. Our new family was so happy together. Victoria learned how to speak English and enrolled in elementary school. She quickly started to enjoy her American life, and we provided her with everything she needed. Victoria's biological dad never contacted her after she came to the US; he never called, sent a Birthday card, or sent any money. In two years, Edward proceeded to adopt Victoria, and she became his daughter.

God blessed me beyond what I ever hoped, beyond what I ever dreamed possible. He gave us Diana, my second baby girl, in 2011. She is sweet and beautiful. And then God gave us Yana in 2015. Her hair is long and blonde, like Elsa's from Frozen. And her cute little face with one blue eye and one green eye could not be more precious to me. All three of my precious girls are my God's blessings!

I am a lucky woman to be married to such an amazing man. Edward's parents taught him respectful manners when he was little, and as a Christian man, he knows in his heart how to respect his wife, mother, sister, and daughter.

In my life, I have encountered many people in their marriages that disrespect one another. They can hide it from the public, but both hearts are broken inside their homes. Where there is no respect, there is disrespect. Disrespect grows over time and sometimes becomes uncontrolled. That can lead to name-calling your spouse, rage, and abuse—verbal or physical. This is why respect is the number one foundation in my marriage. And this message is to every lady who might read this book: don't let your husband disrespect you because love can't be without respect.

One of my favorite verses God teaches us about love and what love truly is. "Love is gentle, love is kind..." As humans, we tend to hold a grudge against people who hurt us. How can we forgive people close to us who have done us wrong?

It is not easy. We always have to give a person who hurt us another chance because God calls us to forgive and keep no records of wrong. And if that person hurts us again, it's time to let go. Let go of a burden and let go of hate. For me, it took years to let go of the hurt from my first husband. And it took several years of praying to God to release me of that hate and hurt in my soul and to receive complete freedom.

Only with the Lord can we get there. Only his supernatural power can release us from deep pain that we drown in alcohol or other substances. Only God can do it for us—but YOU are in charge! You have to ask your Heavenly Father to help you! And I promise He will hear you. He will put you away under his warm comfort of unconditional, deep, and true love and care for you.

I can't tell you how many times I had nightmares about my ex-husband being abusive in my dreams and me waking up scared and crying to God in the middle of the night.

And this is my message to ALL women who were abused. NEVER go back. It is tough to forgive a person who did wrong to you. But eventually, forgiveness in your heart will bring you peace.

Don't waste your time on people who hurt you. God has a plan for you, a better plan like he always does. You just have to believe it and pray about it.

God's love for us will never fail us; he will love us unconditionally if we just follow him.

"LOVE IS PATIENT, LOVE IS KIND. IT DOES NOT ENVY, IT DOES NOT

BOAST, IT IS NOT PROUD.

IT DOES NOT DISHONOR OTHERS, IT IS NOT SELF-SEEKING,

IT IS NOT EASILY ANGERED, IT KEEPS NO RECORD OF WRONGS.

LOVE DOES NOT DELIGHT IN EVIL BUT REJOICES WITH THE TRUTH.

IT ALWAYS PROTECTS, ALWAYS TRUSTS, ALWAYS HOPES,

ALWAYS PERSEVERES"

1 CORINTHIANS 13:4-7

Love Never Fails

REFLECTION

*If anything touches your heart today,
let it flow out, and allow God to work within you
to bring you peace and joy.*

Faith.

I am 43 years old, the same age as my mom passed away. Some would say it's a midlife crisis to write this book. The only way I can explain it is having a strong desire to write about my journey.

In my 20s, I didn't understand my faith in God much. I always knew there was a God, prayed occasionally, and went to Church only for Christmas. The way I grew up in Orthodox and Catholic environments didn't teach me anything. I love attending the Catholic church for a beautiful candlelight Christmas service. I love all the elaborate beauty on the interior of the old church buildings and the sense of many wax candles. However, I didn't seek much to learn and hear God or live an authentic Christian life in those places. In the culture where I am from, most of the people do believe in Jesus. Although they celebrate Christmas on another day in the old calendar, the main idea is the same.

But learning what it means to be a follower of Jesus indeed and live a Christian life is far away from the practices with which I was raised. I've seen many Orthodox people cheat constantly on their wives and live double lives with mistresses. I've seen people mistreat, disrespect, and abuse their wives. I've seen many families that just felt apart: my own family, my brothers' families, my cousin's family, my great aunt's family, and my aunt's family. The causes could be abuse, alcohol, or cheating.

If these people are believers and obey God's word, would that be the results? And I know we all make mistakes, but what we do after those mistakes makes a real difference. Having the Lord in your heart is a foundation for a strong family; when your ship rocks during the storm, you hang on to your faith and pray. The supernatural power of the Holy Spirit pours love on you and comforts you, and the word of God gives you knowledge and wisdom to make the right decision. Jesus died for us and paid for our sins. I also believe that only the Lord's holy spirit, through prayers, can restore your soul.

Being in the USA and attending a non-denominational church for almost nine years, I see the difference in my life. I am so grateful for our local church and our pastor, who inspires me every week and shares the Lord's words, which are easy to understand and apply. I am so thankful for the Bible studies and church groups that allowed me to meet new women and grow spiritually. Now, I can easily understand and relate to a Bible verse and see what God says through it. I never got a chance to do that in an Orthodox church. All I've seen from childhood is a singing priest dressed in fancy clothing and kissing the icons. I am not against it, but from my experience, worship didn't do me any good. In the Catholic church, I had the same experience. I never understood why you must talk to a third person, a priest, to confess your sin. It led nowhere with my spiritual growth and how my family and I lived in Latvia.

I've been going to a Baptist church in the US. I have grown spiritually so much, and I've learned so many amazing things that I apply to my life. I want to share them with my Russian family and friends, but it isn't easy.

If I tell them I go to a Baptist church, they take it the wrong way. Like it's a different religion, sometimes their strong opinions are hard to persuade.

In my personal life, I had an incredible person that brought me closer to the Lord. She was the most wonderful, peaceful woman I have ever met. Her name was Nicolle, my mother-in-law. The first time I met her, I felt right at home. It's that feeling when you enter a house and feel at peace and joy, like close family. She was sweet, gentle and kind. Later, she told Edward that she loved me from the first time she met me. And I loved her, too; she was like my second mom. I could tell her anything.

Nicolle was scared to fly and rarely visited us from LA to Atlanta. But one summer before she passed away, I invited her to come and stay with us for two weeks to help with my baby Diana, who was four months old. She said, "Angelika, I prayed for the Lord to remove my fear of flying, and I think I want to come." And what an incredible two weeks we had. Victoria and I took her shopping and went to get our nails done. We even convinced her to try sushi, which she spit out. We laughed so hard because she had swallowed too much wasabi.

During her visit, she shared with me her own challenging life story. It was so painful to hear it, but God had healed her soul from her pain. She said she didn't even tell her kids in detail. For many years, she struggled to forgive a person, and she prayed to the Lord to heal her heart and bring forgiveness to her soul. And then she said, "One day at a church, I was holding hands with other ladies and praying. Then she heard the voice telling her, 'You are not going to hurt anymore." That was when the Lord released all her pain and hate and set her free. Lord gave her forgiveness and new love toward the person she needed to love again. During those two weeks of her visit, she shared her passion for Jesus with me many times, and her calm presence just brought a sense of peace to our home. She was the most influential woman in my spiritual growth path, but unfortunately, she passed away too soon. I miss her dearly. It hurts so much not to have her in my and my kids' lives. Often, Edward and I talk about how much Nicolle would love seeing our girls and playing with them. What an incredible woman of faith and love.

Betrayal.

During my stay in Riga, I decided to sell the summer home built by my dad. The house needed to be taken care of, and I knew I could not go back to Latvia often to stay there. I felt bad that it required maintenance and was very sad that I had to sell it.

Max's older sister Kate lived in Riga. We had always been in a good relationship and often got together for coffee. She and her husband had a furniture business, and they owned a lovely home outside Riga, an apartment, and nice cars. Overall, their lives were well-established back then.

During my stay in Riga, while we were waiting on Victoria's immigration paperwork, Kate helped me move a few things into the apartment. For the most part, she was on my side and supported me. She brought me an extra sofa to sleep on since the apartment only had one living room and a tiny bed.

Because Victoria and I are going to the USA, I decided to give Kate my power of attorney so she could sell my house and transfer money to me after I left.

After I left with Victoria, the house sold for about $12,000. Kate transferred around $2,000, but I never got the rest of my money. She lied to me that she'd transfer money soon, over and over for a couple of years, but she never did.

I felt betrayed by her. It was my house built by my dad's hands, and she took the money for it. I tried to sue her, but it led nowhere. I prayed to remove my anger and hate toward her and the pain that Kate caused me, and He did. I was able to forgive her, although she never really asked for it. I forgive her for stealing from me.

Later, I discovered her husband left her with three kids. All her properties, car, and business were gone with him, and she had nothing left. God has His way for our life paths.

"The Lord is my light and my salvation;

whom shall I fear?

The Lord is the stronghold of my life;

of whom shall I be afraid?

When evildoers assail me to eat up my flesh,

my adversaries and foes, it is they who stumble and fall.

Though an army encamp against me,

my heart shall not fear;

though war arise against me,

yet I will be confident"

Psalm 27:1-3

REFLECTION

*If anything touches your heart today,
let it flow out, and allow God to work within you
to bring you peace and joy.*

Chapter 6

Friendships

I grew up in Riga, and in the summers, my family would go to a summer home that my dad built. The home was located in a rural area close to the small town of Sigulda.

Our home has been built with Dad's love, and every detail has reflected it. The red brick fireplace highlighted the dining area where we often gathered for dinner and cooked kebabs on the skewers. The wall with mirrors in the living room was from floor to ceiling, nothing fancy, just a loving touch for my beautiful mom. Different wallpaper in every room; yes, it was very common to have it back then. And the most beautiful thing was my dad's ironwork; he made a gate and a balcony rail for the house. I used to love to repaint it with Dad. Also, we had consistently grown a garden with cucumbers, tomatoes, fresh dill, and strawberries. My mom used to do pickles and strawberry jams for winter. The house would smell so delicious with a sweet smell of fresh strawberries.

My friend Sophia lived across the street from my summer house, and we were neighbors during the summer. She had been my best friend since we were little girls and always played together. Sophia was a beautiful blonde girl with amazing blue eyes. In the summertime, we rode bikes, picked mushrooms, and swam with other friends. We've been in each other's life during our first relationships with boys and shared our deepest secrets that no one else knew. She was closer than my friend, more like a sister to me.

Unfortunately, we have not been friends for more than ten years. It still hurts me. I don't cry as often as I used to, but occasionally I still do. The way we said goodbye to each other and our friendship was not a proper way to say goodbye to someone who has been your friend since age four. A person like this is more than a friend; they become a part of who you are. We may not be related by blood, but life connects us. We learned to ride our bikes together, sang songs in our moms' long robes, and created shows for each other. We shared lives, feelings, and hopes during our friendship.

Looking back, I can point out the differences between me and her, and only now, as a mature adult, can I understand that we were very different on the inside.

Sophia moved to the US before me, and I will be forever grateful for her help. She helped me financially when I lived with Maria in Riga and helped me process my student visa to come here to the US, too. Back then, I thought Sophia's life in the US was a piece of cake, but it wasn't. She just never shared her hardships on a deep level. She worked very hard and could afford expensive clothes, and I don't blame her. It's just I was at a different stage of my life. Although I worked hard, too, I couldn't afford much since I had to save money and support Victoria back in Riga. We were just different in our values and life perspectives.

We had our ups and downs in Riga and USA. I reconciled with her after I left my first husband. But after I married Edward and brought Victoria to the US, I felt she didn't care as much about our friendship.

After Edward and I moved to Charleston from Atlanta, we often returned to Atlanta for my daughter's volleyball tournaments. I would have loved to see Sophia, but she never came, which hurt my feelings.

Sophia's 35th birthday party was planned in a cabin 6-7 hours away from Charleston. Edward and I drove with our one-year-old baby Diana all day to get there. I wanted to be there for her, although the trip was difficult. I often felt like my friend wanted everything "the best" at all times, and it became uncomfortable at some points to talk and compare material things like our engagement rings or the value of new strollers for our babies.

Sophia and her family visited us in Charleston for a long weekend one summer. I still don't know what happened that weekend, but she wasn't thrilled around us. Something seemed to be off, and it became uncomfortable to be around her. When we went to a park, she was upset, and when we suggested doing something, she never liked it. Her personality seemed narcissistic. One evening, my husband argued with her because she wanted to go out with her family for dinner, and Edward offered to cook dinner at home so we could all enjoy it. I didn't hear everything that was going on between them, but I knew it wasn't good. The next day, she wasn't talking to Edward or me. Her behavior toward me was distant and cold.

When she and her family were ready to leave, I told her, "Sophia, think about others too sometimes, and not only about yourself." Later that day, I received a bitter and mean email pointing out my flaws, my betrayal of her, and how she helped me when I was in Riga by sending money to me and my baby so I wouldn't die from hunger.

I didn't hold back and told her how I felt about everything and her behavior, although I should've calmed down before I responded. Her response in her next email broke off our friendship. She said she didn't want to be friends any longer and blocked me on Facebook.

What hurts the most is that we never got to explain our feelings and thoughts face to face. A few months later, I saw she was pregnant and had a baby shower without inviting me. I knew then that I had no place in her life anymore.

In a recent church service, our pastor said if a relationship is valuable to you, it is worth fighting for. I wanted to return to Sophia and say, *"I am very sorry, and let's forgive each other and move on,"* but I wasn't sure how Sophia would perceive that. I felt like Sophia would blame me for everything on me because I apologized to her first. Then I thought, what's there for me and my family anyway? Is there genuine love and care, or just an obligation to an old friend? Yes, it still hurts to think about her, and I am sad that my childhood friend is no longer there for me.

We both moved on. Since our fight, she has had two more kids, and I have had one. We are not in each other's lives, but I can't help but think of her often. I pray about it and wait for God to show me my path for whatever happens between us because how we said our goodbyes wasn't proper. I pray for her family and well-being and wish her the best.

This morning, I came back from my Wednesday morning bible study group. This will be the 3rd study I went through with the leader, Nelli. And today, I want to put it in writing on how much goodness she brings to our weekly discussion table. She also surrounds all the ladies with her genuine care, understanding, and love. I have known her for three years, and having her in my life has been such a blessing. I know I can tell her everything and will be heard and not judged, and I'll be prayed for. I thank the Lord for bringing her into my life. I can honestly say that without having this group of such extraordinary ladies, I wouldn't have the support I needed to return to Riga and take Victoria to see Lydia and Max in the summer of 2019. I would not have had the courage and wisdom to handle that trip. Even better, I wouldn't have started to write this memoir. Her friendship is a blessing to me.

We all go through different seasons of our lives, and it is so important to have your support system. I know which friends and people I want to be surrounded with.

Recently, I talked about friendships with Victoria, my oldest daughter, who is having difficulty handling the Nursing Degree in her junior year in college, plus volleyball season and personal life. I told her, "Please, please, surround yourself with friends who uplift your spirit. Not the ones that will bring you down and make you feel bad and unhappy. But the ones that will bring you a light in the dark days, with their care." Sometimes, we go through difficult seasons, and I think friends play a significant role. Good friends are hard to find. As we go through life and grow spiritually, our friends change as we change. Friends can drag you down emotionally, too. So my advice to my daughters and other girls is that if a friendship doesn't feel right, don't force it. Pray about it and let it go. The sooner you realize that a particular person is not suitable for you, the better it is for you. God knows your heart and will close one door and open another.

God truly blessed me with my new friends here in Charleston. They are all immigrants, too, and speak Russian, although they are not from Riga. I love them all. We laugh together and share our difficult moments as well. Each of them adds something different to my life in a good way. I love how open we can be with each other without any judgments.

There is another dear friend of mine that I met in Charleston, and we have known each other for almost ten years now. She has three young girls similar in age to my two younger kids. She is a super fun, strong, and creative woman. I connect with her as we share the same passion for creativity and try to raise our girls to be good kids. I love her dearly, and I know God put her in my life with all her love for me and my family. I am forever grateful for it. She is a fantastic person.

Each person in our lives serves a purpose, and we serve a purpose in their lives. Often, we really can't explain why certain things happen the way they do, but only God knows. We don't need to know. Having a good friend is a gift from God, and we need to treasure these people in our lives. I am very blessed to have a few very close friends by my side who are Russian-speaking; we can laugh together, cry together, and share our secrets. I love those ladies dearly.

"THE HEARTFELT COUNSEL OF A FRIEND

IS AS SWEET

AS PERFUME AND INCENSE"

PROVERB 28:9

REFLECTION

If anything touches your heart today,
let it flow out, and allow God to work within you
to bring you peace and joy.

Chapter 7

Children

In the United States, it is often perceived that to have a baby before 21 is a teen pregnancy. In other countries, women usually get married in their early 20s. But no matter where you live, laws and opinions can't determine the right age to have a baby. Looking back on my life, I agree that 19 is too early to have a child. But, as I grow in my faith, I believe my pregnancy with my oldest daughter, Victoria, was a gift from God.

I remember the day I missed my period and went to the OBGYN. I hated that medical facility and was embarrassed to wait in a long line in the hallway to see the doctor. At that time, I was only in 11th grade. When my time came, I shook like a leaf in the wind when the doctor was checking me. She said, short and fast, "You are 4-6 weeks along. Are you having an abortion or keeping the baby?" The only words I said were, "Oh my word," and I started to cry. I did not plan this and did not know what to do. How could I go back home to my grandma Maria and tell her I was pregnant? I knew she would disgrace me forever.

The doctor said to come back in a few days with my decision about whether I wanted to keep the baby. I called my boyfriend Max, who lived in Russia at that time. He was quiet at first and then said, "OK, we just need to get married." A couple of months later, he came back from Russia, and we planned a marriage stamp registration in the local government office. I was seven months pregnant and had a huge belly.

I wore a white dress that was not intended to be a "wedding dress," and I felt very unattractive. A small wedding and a party at home with a few friends. There is nothing like girls now of a wedding with bridesmaids and their prince charming. But at that time, I was happy. It was my happiness to carry my baby under my heart and to look forward to something in my life. A new family member was a blessing after my parents' passing. My relationship with my grandmother, Maria, had always been challenging. She never liked Max and told me I was unwise to keep the baby. We didn't speak for months. Just before I married, my grandma and I finally started talking again.

Not only was my pregnancy perceived as a problem by my high school teachers, nosy neighbors, and some friends, but it was also hard financially.

It was 1998-1999, a challenging year for Latvia. It wasn't easy to find a job. I wasn't working at all and was trying to finish high school. We lived with my grandmother in a small Stalin-era apartment with one bedroom and a living room where my grandmother slept. We didn't have money to support our new family. The only money we had to buy something new for my baby was 10 dollars. I remember going to the kid's store and buying a yellow plush baby blanket and a light green blanket cover to bring my baby home from the hospital. I didn't know the baby's gender since they didn't offer this service back then.

Some friends gave me an old stroller with huge old-fashioned wheels, which I was so happy about because it was free. Some other people brought me two bags of used baby clothes, which was such a blessing. The Bible says, "God will provide," and God did provide for me, just what I needed.

Despite my poor life, Victoria, my precious and amazing girl, was a gift. When you were born, you brought my happiness back into my life. After my loss of both parents two years prior, I finally felt God's love again. The joy of holding you in my hands and seeing you grow daily fulfilled and completed me. I have never in my life looked back and regretted it. I always knew deep inside of me that it was meant to be. I am who I am today because of you. You pushed me to reach for new beginnings, set new goals, and pursue a better life. I often think, *What if I didn't have you?*" And with that thought comes a dark cloud of sadness and despair. And by now, I probably would be one of them, living and putting up with a cruel husband and never even achieving anything in my life. So, you, my darling, are the greatest blessing in my life, and I love you dearly.

Fast-forward, and now you are a junior in college. My baby girl, I am so proud of you.

What a wave of excitement and joy you bring to me. At your last volleyball game, you played so hard. You kept pounding that ball down with your strength and power. The waves of excitement went through the audience. It feels incredible to watch you becoming such a strong athlete. I am so proud of you for not giving up on your passion. When you were a freshman at a local High School, I remember how nervous you were about attending varsity tryouts. We all knew how tough it was. But Edward has always been your biggest volleyball fan and supporter. He kept telling you, "Victoria, you can do it; you have all the physical ability, and you are good."

Your dream to play on varsity your junior year was crushed when you didn't make the team. I hated seeing you cry that day. I know how much you wanted it, and it hurt me as much as it hurt you.

But Dad and I kept telling you, "Don't give up. Don't let anyone tell you that you are not good enough." We kept reminding you, "Keep going, and practice on your travel team so you can try again in your senior year." But you hated returning to try it out the following year, and God had a different plan for you.

I was walking in the neighborhood with my baby girl one day, and a truck drove by. He stopped close to me, rolled down the window, and said, "Hello, do you know where the new high school will be around here?" I said, "I didn't even know there was going to be one!" As he drove away, I wondered if a new high school would exist. So I rushed back home and Googled it. I was pleasantly surprised that, indeed, there would be a new Charter High School built nearby. Not only that, but it would also be geared toward student-athletes! I knew it would not be built until Victoria graduated, but I found out the temporary campus would be set up in a small historic town 30 minutes away, and the bus would be provided for students to get there and back. Student-athletes will have half-day classes. I called the school, asked for an admission package, and was thrilled to share my news with Edward. We were unsure that Victoria would want to switch schools in her Senior year. We asked her to think and pray about it, carefully considering the opportunity.

Then Victoria came to us one day and said, "Mom, I want to go to that new school." I always pray for my kids to be safe, healthy, and wise in all they do. Her decision overjoyed Edward and me, and what a blessed senior year she had! It was the best decision a high school girl who dreamed of playing varsity volleyball could have made! The Lord showed that he can place random people into our lives that will affect us. The more I grow in my spiritual life, the more I pray and believe, and the more easily I can recognize these signs from the Lord. So, I encourage you to look around and believe that God can do anything.

"Therefore I tell you, do not be anxious about your life,

what you will eat or what you will drink,

nor about your body, what you will put on.

Is not life more than food, and the body more than clothing?

Look at the birds of the air; they neither sow nor reap nor

gather into barns, and yet your heavenly Father feeds them.

Are you not of more value than they?"

Matthew 6:25

REFLECTION

*If anything touches your heart today,
let it flow out, and allow God to work within you
to bring you peace and joy.*

Chapter 8

Forgiveness

Over the years, my relationship with Lydia (Victoria's grandma in Riga) was on and off. After Pavel passed away, she started calling Victoria and me more often. In the past few years, we have gotten closer, texting pictures to each other. I felt like we had a new start in our relationship, and Lydia often begged me to come to Latvia and stay with her at her summer house and forget all that's happened between us.

I prayed for a long time to be clear about visiting Lydia. In 2019, I had a strong urge to go to Latvia and decided to take Victoria to Riga to visit Lydia and meet Max for the first time since she was three years old.

I keep asking myself the same question: why did I have such a strong desire to return to Latvia last summer? The most important thing was that Lydia asked me to come so Max and Victoria could start a relationship. Victoria wanted to give it a shot, and Edward and I fully supported Victoria's desire. At first, I didn't want to do it. I wouldn't say I liked that idea. It took me a few years of praying over it and letting the Lord be in control of it before I could go back. I prayed for God to remove my hate from my heart. I prayed for the Lord to give me the courage and wisdom to make the right decision about the trip. Although I took Victoria back to see Lydia twice after moving to the US, Victoria never saw Max in person. They only started to communicate when she turned 18.

Finally, I decided I was going, and my daughters went with me. If Lydia was so friendly to my girls and me, I wanted to give her a chance to be in my life again and in my girls' lives since they don't have a grandma anyway. I have known this woman for over 20 years, and visiting her is the least I can do to show her grace for helping me raise Victoria. I felt I owed it to her to see what a wonderful young lady Victoria had become. Lydia reassured me that during my stay in her summer house, Max wouldn't bother or come to visit us. I ensured Lydia knew that I didn't want to meet with him either since we had nothing to say to each other. But I agreed that Max and Victoria could meet and start their relationship if they chose to do so. I won't be against it.

Lydia was extremely excited when I booked my tickets for our trip. I planned to stay with my younger kids at Lydia's place for four weeks. Then Victoria would come for a fifth week. Lydia said that Max was also planning it and would take her around the city to show her places, take her to a concert, and take her shopping for nice clothes. It all sounded too good to be true. I am grateful that God gave me some wisdom to prepare my daughter to meet her biological father mentally. I said, "Victoria, please set your expectations to zero. Please don't expect anything. Don't expect a caring, loving person. He wasn't like that for 20 years—not a single birthday card or phone call, so I doubt it will magically happen when he sees you."

When I arrived, I stayed at Lydia's summer house, and we had a great time together. I was able to bring some new things for her house to make her happy. I cleaned the house's attic space and swept away the spider webs and mouse dirt before Victoria arrived. I listened to Lydia complain about her grandkids not visiting or calling her often and how her own daughter Kate hardly cared about her. I felt so bad for her.

My only prayer during my stay was for God to keep me and my girls safe there and give me lots of grace. I stayed there for four weeks before Victoria came. I enjoyed taking my girls around the old city to museums and showing them where I grew up. I also visited my dad's summer house and surprisingly didn't cry when I saw it. It looked very different but in a good way. I was glad to see that the home my dad built was well cared for by the people who bought it.

When Victoria got to Riga, we went to Lydia's old apartment complex. Nothing had changed since I last saw it, still grey, worn-down Stalin-era five-story flat apartments. It reminded me how sad my old life looked, but I kept all the comments inside out of respect to my ex-mother-in-law. As we slowly walked up the stairs to the fourth floor, flashbacks from my past followed. I remember dragging the heavy, old-fashioned stroller up and down when Victoria was a baby. I also remembered the time I was found unconscious Pavel, lying on the stairway floor drunk.

A new, lovely front door led to the old days. We walked into the small foyer with the same mirror and some art. It appeared so tiny. The two rooms, which used to be large living rooms and master bedrooms, were utterly gutted. There was no furniture or any sign of remodeling—only some samples of flooring and miscellaneous items lying around. I spotted the large balcony I loved reading on and rocking Victoria as a baby. It wasn't clean, and I saw some empty bottles of alcohol. The kitchen was always tiny and appeared in better shape with a few updates. Victoria's third bedroom was where she lived with Lydia all five years. It was nothing like we remembered, but the silk, airy blue curtains remained. They had been my curtains when I lived with my grandmother, and I loved them. We didn't have many nice things back then, and I always remembered what I had in Riga. So it had been seventeen years since I lived there, and Max still had those curtains. As we explored the apartment, Victoria saw a few pictures that he had of her. She said it looked so different from what she remembered. So we left and closed the heavy door behind us.

Victoria's elementary school was the next stop, where she went for first and second grades. It was a five-minute drive between neighborhood streets. There is usually one building in the schools that combines kindergarten through high school. The building appeared nicely updated, with a new playground behind it. We decided to go inside and see it. Her childhood memories refreshed her mind, and she told me, "Mom, thank you for taking me away from here. I could never imagine living here in the old apartment and finishing at this school." Victoria was overwhelmed. She was only in Riga for a week and was ready to return home to the US on our second day. I saw in Victoria's eyes how shocked she was to see her childhood apartments and school and how grateful she was for not growing up there. My soul was hurting to see this grey life again, but the profound gratefulness overwhelmingly covered me. I felt so grateful for my life and Victoria's life, which is different now. I am very thankful that the Lord has abundantly provided for both of us.

After a few days in Riga, Max called. I kept reminding myself to give him another chance to establish his relationship with Victoria. Victoria and Max were supposed to meet for lunch on the fourth day. I couldn't sleep that night since all the ugly and evil thoughts from our past were coming out. It was scary, and I knew evil was steering my heart toward rage. I prayed, turning in my bed repeatedly, "Lord, please get the evil away from me, Lord. I don't want it in my heart. Jesus, please let me not have fear again, please Jesus." It was an emotional battle that evil would win if I allowed it.

The following day, I woke up and wasn't sure if I needed to see Max when I dropped off Victoria to meet him. I prayed, "Lord, let it be your will." Once we were pulling into the car parking lot, where he was supposed to meet Victoria, nothing in my heart shook. No part of my body was shaking like it used to in fear of this man. Victoria said, "Mom, I can't go alone. You are coming with me." We parked the car and walked over. As we both walked toward Max, I secretly rejoiced. I had done my hair and makeup the best I could that morning. I wore a cute summer blue dress with comfortable flip-flops and topped it off confidently. I said, "Victoria, this is Max. Max, this is Victoria." That was all I could find to say. It was an empty feeling to meet him again after so many years. My tongue could not find any words, no bad, no good. He appeared much smaller and skinnier than I remembered him. No longer was he big and robust, like when I was 20. My past fears of him were defeated, my hate was gone, and my pride was deleted from my heart. The only feeling in my heart today is feeling sorry for this man.

Victoria called me to pick her up an hour and a half later since they were done with lunch. I asked her how it went, and she said it was alright since they didn't have much to discuss. But then she added, " He asked me if I wanted to meet his girlfriend and her kids. I said no, not yet." She added, "Mom, I have no interest in meeting them now. Maybe later in life, but not now." I told her, "Yes, I agree, and I always want you to follow your heart and whatever feels right to you."

After that meeting, we went back to Lydia's place. She had changed. We could tell she wasn't happy about Victoria not wanting to see Max's future wife and kids. Victoria cried in the room that evening. She said, "Mom, I can't stand this anymore. Grandmother pushes me to meet them, but I don't want to." I left my room and politely said, "Lydia, with all due respect, Victoria doesn't want to do it yet. I suggest Max focus on Victoria only for now and spend one-on-one time with her to try rebuilding their relationship."

After that, Max didn't call or try to see Victoria again. We were there for another five days, and he did nothing. Since he did not like Victoria's answer, his ego and pride were hurt. He could not overcome it. And look how it affected him. Only weeks later, Victoria told me he had texted her when we were on the plane leaving Riga. He said, "Victoria, I am so sorry I didn't meet with you again. As soon as I saw your mom, all the bad times came up in my memory, and I could not handle it. I love you, daughter."

I know Victoria will remember this for a long time. Max let evil continue the work in his life. Evil continued to keep him in the same place for many years with anger, bitterness, and self-pity. Pride has been living comfortably with Max for 20 years. I won't judge anything he has done to me. I left that part to the Lord. But I've seen his pride ruining his life; sadly, he doesn't understand it.

God's blessing shined again through this challenging trip. Victoria understood much more about what it meant to have a real dad. Edward raised her with his unconditional love, respect, and wisdom. If nothing else, the Lord showed her who loves her. I am forever grateful to God for sending me such an incredible man who loves Victoria unconditionally and as deeply as his child.

A few days after we came home, Lydia texted me and told me that she fully supported her son in how he handled Victoria's visit and wished me good luck in life. I was stunned. It's not how we said our goodbyes at her house. Lydia was crying when we left and promised that she would try to attend Victoria's graduation in 2021. But something changed, and it hurt me again. Again, I felt so betrayed by this family. I felt naive for allowing myself to trust Lydia again. After everything that we had for four weeks together without issues, I felt unloved. It broke my heart, especially for my little daughters, who felt Lydia's love during our visit, and my heart hurt for Victoria, too.

I sacrificed so much time and money to buy tickets to fly overseas, rent a car, and live there for so long, only just to get stabbed in the back after I left.

But God surprised me with a little reward. On our flight back, my flight was delayed for a day, and I had submitted for a refund. A few weeks later, the airline refunded our tickets almost 80%, more than $2,000! I cried for joy, not because I got my money back but because it felt like God was giving me his little gift and saying, "It's ok, you did what I needed you to do, so here is something back for you to make you feel better."

"For if you forgive other people when

they sin against you, your heavenly

Father will also forgive you"

Matthew 6:14

REFLECTION

*If anything touches your heart today,
let it flow out, and allow God to work within you
to bring you peace and joy.*

Chapter 9

Life today

Sometimes, I wonder why God created me as I am. Why do I have so many feelings? I just want to stop feeling sometimes. I want to put my feelings in a small bottle and throw them away into a deep ocean where they can sink so I don't have to feel them anymore.

I wish I could finish this as a "happily ever after story." That would be almost true, but I know it wouldn't be honest. I made a long pause to continue writing this book. For several months, I had no desire to open this file. We have had a lockdown since March 2020 for the COVID-19 pandemic, so today is my children's long-awaited first day of face-to-face school. Not only that but there have also been other struggles and soul-searching lately.

Today, I mark two months of alcohol-free life since I had my last glass of wine. Oh, how I loved my wine! I was becoming even more defensive about sharing it with my husband. In the endless days of lockdown during Covid-19, I could not go a day without it. How else would I be able to handle all my fears, uncertainties, and isolation from my everyday life? So, boxed wine was the solution in my house until it didn't feel good anymore. Until I could not numb my sadness and what started to feel like depression. I woke up at 3 am every morning for no reason and rarely slept well. In the morning, when I looked at myself in the mirror, I hated my face, even if I had only one or two glasses of wine the night before. My mood was affected almost every morning, and I felt inside that something was not right.

I tried to limit my intake but caught myself thinking on Mondays, "Is it Friday yet?" There were anxious nights when I could not wait to put my kids to bed so I could pour a glass of wine, enjoy my time alone, and forget my unhappy existence during the lockdown. My mind has been racing for a long time now. How can I feel so sad if I have everything I ever dreamed of and God blessed me beyond what I ever imagined? Why am I feeling this way? Why am I so irritable with my kids and my spouse? And why don't I even want to do the job I love?

My hands did not want to do anything any longer, and my spirit was battling a sneaky devil. The one that comes and says, "You are not worthy. You are a failure. You don't need to be happy. You are no one. You are a sinner."

And Lord, you are still so good to me! Today, I want to scream at the top of my lungs that my strength always comes from you. I can cry and pour my heart out in prayer, and you will always hear me. No fancy words, just the honest, humble mumbling of my soul. In this life, you will have troubles...many! I am so grateful that God always has a plan for us.

A book that my friend recommended to me two months ago changed me and released me from wanting wine or other alcohol. It was not even hard to quit.

If you are reading these words and are curious, here is the book I suggest that will clear your mind: "Kick the Drink Easily" by Jason Vale. Amazingly, God put this book into the hands of my good friend, and now my other two friends and I are alcohol-free. God is so good! I know he has great plans for each of us.

"NOTHING IS IMPOSSIBLE WITH GOD"

MATTHEW 1:37

REFLECTION

If anything touches your heart today,
let it flow out, and allow God to work within you
to bring you peace and joy.

The End

Finding the inspiration and wisdom to write this book has been difficult. Life is too busy with COVID-19, everyday life of taking care of kids and family, cooking, cleaning, and doing freelance work.

But when God puts something on your heart, he will not let you go. One day, while sitting in a writing class, I saw a hummingbird fly fast to the large window before me. An overwhelming warm feeling of seeing that bird came to my heart. My sweet mother-in-law Nicolle used to adore hummingbirds. Right then and there, I knew it was God's sign that I wanted to pursue writing this book.

As I am still growing in my faith, it is delightful to recognize the minor signs around me. They appear randomly, and I know God is with me.

It is May 2024, and I am eager to publish this book. I hope this story will inspire my readers.

A story of a simple girl who lost her parents so young. A young girl who chose another life over abortion. A young girl who struggled with an abusive relationship. A young girl who had an abortion. A young girl who left her country hoping to find a better life. A young girl who suffered five long years without seeing her child. A young lady who was forgiven by the grace of God. And finally, a woman who always believed in Jesus as her Lord and Savior. A woman who got up on her feet and went to college. A woman who opened her own business. A woman who has a wonderful family and is abundantly blessed financially, personally, and spiritually. And I give all my thanks and glory to the Lord for all he has done for me. And I know he can do it for you.

Thank you for reading this book. Let this book inspire you wherever you are in your life. Let God's story give you new hope. May your renewed faith overcome any unhappiness in your life. Put your trust in God and pray about everything. Be humble and dream big. Be supportive of other people and give grace. Be kind, and don't ever give up. Don't let anyone mistreat you; never forget who you are.

Conclusion

I believed my life was meant for evil since my dad didn't want me. I remember my grandmother told me this. And she also told me a story that my dad told my mother: he said he'd leave her if she kept me. My mom had numerous abortions before me; so much sin and hurt before I was even born.

They also dealt with my father's sin and the curse he had on his first wife when he left her pregnant. She had a late abortion and cursed my dad for what he had done to her.

But I am still here on this earth. I truly believe God's grace was given to me after I turned my life toward Jesus. And all my dad's and mom's sins were forgiven and washed away. Only our Lord can do it. Only He can grant us new joy and peace by forgiving us for our actions. It is God's gift of forgiveness.

I miss my dad and mom every day. I still don't know why God took them away from me at such a young age, but I hope they are both in a better place. It took me 22 years to hear God's answer that my dad went to heaven. It took me 20 years to reflect on God's story that he weaved in my life. And this book is not about my life but our gracious heavenly Father who loves us unconditionally.

I pray that Jesus guides my spirit to write the words that are needed for you, my readers. It is not easy to write about my sins, my pain, and my mistakes. But the bigger picture of how GOOD our God is makes it well worth it. It is because of Jesus, who lives in me and guides me, that I feel a need to honor him and shout out to the world, "Lord, you are good!"

Believe it; believe in Christ with every inch of your body, every dark spot of your broken soul. Believe that Jesus IS our King, and if we follow him, he will NEVER let us down. He will meet all of our needs and heal our deepest wounds. He is a powerful and everlasting God. Don't fear life's problems, sickness, or death. Rejoice in His presence of peace and your heart every day. Jesus is near. He is here. In my soul, forever.

God Bless You All. May His peace be with you and angels cover you under their wings.

"I HAVE TOLD YOU THESE THINGS,

SO THAT IN ME YOU MAY HAVE PEACE.

IN THIS WORLD YOU WILL HAVE TROUBLE.

BUT TAKE HEART!

I HAVE OVERCOME THE WORLD."

JOHN 16:33

REFLECTION

If anything touches your heart today,
let it flow out, and allow God to work within you
to bring you peace and joy.

Printed in the United States
by Baker & Taylor Publisher Services